The Wound

The Wound

JOHN KINSELLA

Poems after *Buile Suibhne*
and Friedrich Hölderlin

Arc
PUBLICATIONS
2018

Published by Arc Publications
Nanholme Mill, Shaw Wood Road,
Todmorden OL14 6DA, UK
www.arcpublications.co.uk

978 1910345 97 9 (pbk)
978 1910345 98 6 (hbk)
978 1910345 99 3 (ebk)

ACKNOWLEDGEMENTS
Some of these poems have previously been published in
Hampden-Sydney Poetry Review, Meanjin, Mutually Said (a blog
John Kinsella shares with Tracy Ryan), *Overland, Salzburg Review,
Stop the War Coalition* website, *The Wolf* and *York Community
Matters Newspaper.*
Special thanks to Andrée Gerland and to the Literary
Cultures of the Global South programme, University of
Tübingen, Germany, where the author was in residence for some
months during 2016. Special thanks too to all at Arc Publications
– James Byrne, Jean Boase-Beier, Tony Ward and Angela Jarman.
The author has had a special interaction with Arc for over two
decades, and appreciates the rigorous attention they have always
given his work as well as the personal support he has received
from them. Further thanks to Curtin University and Churchill
College, Cambridge University.

Cover image: © Stephen Kinsella, 2018,
by kind permission of the artist.

Editor for Arc's International Poets series
James Byrne

For Tracy, Tim,
the 'Save Beeliar Wetlands' protesters,
Andrée, and James Quinton

CONTENTS

Introduction / 9

BOOK ONE – AFTER SWEENEY

Sweeney Prototype (Outdoors, West Cork) / 15
Sweeney the Vegan / 17
Sweeney's Lament / 23
Sweeney's Remedy for Bathos / 24
Graphology Chronotype 3: Sweeney / 26
Sweeney Deplores Nationalism in the Hazy Days of Summer / 27
Sweeney in the Hawthorn Tree Confused by
Hiberno-Australian-English / 28
Sweeney Suffers at the Paws of the Otter / 31
Sweeney's Flight of Exile / 33
A Charred Sweeney Arises, Brainwashed by the State, to Imprint
Himself on the Locals Taking up Their Racist Desires / 35
Is it Hubris with which Sweeney Awaits
the Approach of a Double Front? / 37
Sweeney – 'Little Birdie Flying High' – Shits on a Gathering of
Crypto-Fascists but Means Nothing Aggressive by It / 38
The Tenets or Tenants of Sweeney / 39
Sweeney – Bird Brain Dissembler / 40
Sweeney the Thesaurus Bird / 41
Sweeney Encounters a Russian Adventurer
in the Avon Valley / 43
Sweeney Deplores the Rise of the Fascists / 45
Sweeney Tries to Warn Locals of the Danger of
a Radioactive Waste Dump / 47
Sweeney Goes to Sing 'All Things Bright and Beautiful'
but No Sound Issues Forth / 49
Sweeney Contemplates a Display of Force
by the Police State / 50
Sweeney Inside the Wound, the Graveyard, the Deathzone / 52
Sweeney the Barn Owl Opens His Eyes Wide in Broad Daylight / 53
Sweeney's Last Will and Testament / 54

Sweeney Witnesses the Attack on the Coolbellup Bush
by the Forces of a Corrupt Police State / 55
Having Given Up the Ghost, Sweeney Flies in with
Seedlings to Help Stitch the Wound / 57
Sweeney Dreams He's Having a Nightmare of Clearing / 58

INTERLUDE

The Old Professors Try to Knock Sweeney Off His Perch
in the Hölderlinturm / 63

BOOK TWO – AFTER HÖLDERLIN

After 'Friedensfeier' / 67
Flames after Hölderlin: Wenn über dem Weinberg / 72
Barely Hölderlin's 'Vom Abgrund nemlich' / 73
Subtexting 'Der Spaziergang' / 75
Searching 'Der Spaziergang' / 76
Winter: Artificial Lake Heading Towards Meltdown / 77
Inverting 'Geh unter, schöne Sonne' / 78
Hölderlin's 'Abendphantasie' and the Unwelcomings of *Here* / 79
Reaching into 'Des Morgens' / 80
In lieblicher Bläue? / 81
Oedipus Speaks: after Hölderlin's *Sophocles' Oedipus*
Second Act Scene One Opening Speech / 82
Messenger: after the Fifth Speech of the Messenger,
Act 1, Scene 3 of Hölderlin's *Sophocles' Antigone* / 84
After Hölderlin's 'Der Winkel vont Hahrdt' / 86
Fantasia on Hölderlin's 'Hälfte des Lebens' / 87
Fantasia (2) on Hölderlin's 'Hälfte des Lebens' / 88
Fantasia (3) on Hölderlin's 'Hälfte des Lebens' / 89
Listening to Nirvana and Working With Andree Gerland's
'Literal' Version of Hölderlin's 'Hälfte des Lebens' / 90
After Hölderlin's Pindar Extravaganza When He Was
Supposedly Past It: 'Das Unendliche' ('The Infinite') / 91

After Hölderlin's Pindar Extravaganza When He Was Supposedly
Past It: 'Vom Delphin' / 92
After Hölderlin's Pindar Extravaganza When He Was
Supposedly Past It: 'Das Belebende' / 93
After 'Der Sommer' – 'Wenn dann vorbei' des
Frühlings Blüthe schwindet / 95
Hymn of Beyond Hölderlin's 'Wie Meeresküsten…'? / 96
We, Too – after Hölderlin's 'Wenn aus dem Himmel / 97
Distance is How We (dis)Orientate: After
'Wenn aus der Ferne…' / 99

Biographical Note / 101

The Wound is two short books in conversation with each other, making a single but pluralistic response to the violence being enacted by humans on humans, and on the natural environment. The Wound is a conversation about peace out of the wounds we have inflicted on the planet in our rapacity and greed, our consumer obsessions.

The literal 'wound' refers to the horrendous gouge in unique coastal bushland in the Beeliar Wetlands and surroundings enacted by the Western Australian conservative Liberal Party-National Party former coalition government under leader Colin Barnett as part of the absurd Roe 8 Highway Extension project in Perth. Having caused much damage, the Barnett government was ousted from power in March 2017, resulting in a cessation of clearing and destruction, but the need for vigilance is a permanent thing. Other bushland at Golden Bay near Perth has been cleared, with BHP [the Anglo-Australian multinational mining, metals and petroleum company] making ready to destroy over 16,000 hectares of habitat to extend their mining operations in the Pilbara, Western Australia. The struggle for the environment is ongoing, and permanent. The assault by the Trump administration on 'wilderness', 'monuments' and coastal waters in the USA, the burning of furze and destruction of hedgerows in Ireland, and the struggle to preserve woodland in the UK, are part of a grim reality of global destruction.

To confront this reality, I have remagined Sweeney, the 'mad king' damned by St. Rónán, suffering as a bird but also bizarrely visionary in a world of warfare and vengeance, emerging out of the wound with visions, epiphanies, revelations, and insistences. The Sweeney poems are entirely my own poems but bounce off the original Irish (anti) epic poem, playing with cycles of motifs and plot mechanisms, with allusions to early Irish poetry in form and gesture. The text distantly followed was Buile Suibhne (The Frenzy of Suibhne), being the adventures of Subhne Geilt, a Middle Irish romance translated by J. G. O'Keeffe, the 1913 edition of which

9

I read online (https://celt.ucc.ie/published/T302018/index.html). I also looked at the 1975 OUP printed edition in the Dublin Institute for Advanced Studies.

A number of the Sweeney poems appeared on the blog I keep with Tracy Ryan, *Mutually Said*, as part of a pacifist resistance against the rapacious assault on the Western Australian environment by government and industry during the Roe 8 debacle already mentioned, the 'Cathedral Avenue' roadside tree clearing wherein the Main Roads Department of Western Australia destroyed ancient old growth trees as part of road-widening – they could have reduced the speed limit for safety – and other 'clearing' of bushland and forest, especially in the Western Australian wheatbelt which now has less than four percent of its original vegetation. Many of these poems are written in support of protesters at the Beeliar Wetlands and on the York-Quairading Road, such as the wonderful Lindsay McNeill who resisted until the last tree was felled and after.

It should be said that I am not Sweeney – Sweeney is many-beaked and becomes many people and animals. He is a bestiary entire in himself, and a litmus paper testing the waters, airs, and soils of country, of conflict, of bigotry, of life, hope and redemption.

The primary text followed in the writing of the Hölderlin poems was the bilingual masterwork, Michael Hamburger's *Friedrich Hölderlin: Poems and Fragments* (trans. Michael Hamburger; 4th Edition, Anvil Press, 2004). I read and 'interacted with' David Constantine's energetic translation, *Hölderlin's Sophocles: Oedipus and Antigone* (Bloodaxe Books, 2001). I also made use of a literal translation of 'Half of Life' by Andrée Gerland and acknowledge my long discussions on Hölderlin with Andrée in Tübingen, plus his gift of *Friedrich Hölderlin: Hälfte des Lebens with an essay by Jochen Schmidt* (Verlag der Buchhandlung Zimmermann, 2008). Other sources include Hölderlin material held in the Hölderlin Tower collection in Tübingen, plus the various German editions of his work that crossed my path (and were used more for 'shape' and 'flow' than literal translation purposes, a task which belongs to a 'translator' *per se*, rather than a poet deeply affected by the idea of the originals as much as the actual texts).

My purpose is always peace, and these poems are written in the brutal shadows of the conflict in Syria, and the bombing by major powers. These are a pacifist response to conflict. They are also a pacifist response to the destruction of country and an affirmation of Indigenous land rights, especially Aboriginal land rights in Australia. I wish to acknowledge the traditional custodians of the 'Western Australian' lands I write – the Ballardong Noongar and Whadjuk Noongar peoples. I acknowledge Elders past, present, and future.

Just a few extra words regarding the poems responding to Hölderlin's Sophocles translations / versions as they are notorious in translation circles because of their oddness and 'errors' re the original (the version he used was also likely suspect according to David Constantine). But maybe even odder in this case because I have had Constantine's effort at rendering a version into English constantly in mind as I've run rampant with the poems-plays to recreate something purposefully *deconstructive* (yes, I mean that precisely). Constantine writes in his introduction to the Bloodaxe versions of *Oedipus* and *Antigone*: 'I kept close to his strange German, in the hope of arriving at an analogous strangeness in English. But his language is beautiful and troubling too, and in carrying over much of that will be lost like precious water from a leaky vessel.' It's this translation loss that delights me and that, for me, creates entry points and exits, voids and holes to weave through – in the slippages the new poem comes that is a splintered reflection of an original lost through translation of translation and (re)versioning of this.

This is a book of political resistance against militarism, environmental destruction, colonialism, xenophobia, racism and fascism spoken out of the wound/s.

John Kinsella, December 2017

11

BOOK ONE
After Sweeney

SWEENEY PROTOTYPE (OUTDOORS, WEST CORK)

To be wild here you only
Have to dissent from identity –
Don't drink from the piss pot,
Don't love but damn the Church.

Welcome strangers to your patch
Of turf, don't hack turf into sods
To burn until the village chokes.
Replant wild land without subsidies.

Don't shoot the fox nor drain the cow,
Lampoon traditions of pollution;
Accept that you will likely be
Strung up at the crossroads.

Claim the glory of a grey wagtail – yellow bird –
So rare in winter even twitchers
Will say 'mis-sighting', 'misattribution',
When you know you're right.

Accept the wisdom of two-pot
Screamers, welcome the blowback,
'Or worse', a foreigner – accept ex-
Communication from entire townlands.

To say, 'There's asbestos and danger',
To read W. B. Yeats by moonlight.
Ignore: 'We don't do that in Ireland!'
And let the rumour of dam*nation* fester.

Love white swans and red sandstone,
Count the ridges of Barnancleeve,
Wish you were stranded on Fastnet,
Soar higher than the gannet.

Yell at the shit-spreader,
Spit slurry out of intensive piggeries,
Co-habit with a quiet but fiery woman
Who will keep gossip to herself.

SWEENEY THE VEGAN

They say I am mad,
out of my tree, as I eat
fruits and nibble leaves,
harvest nuts and make tempeh.

As a teenager I played war games
and dreamed of being a general.
I collected guns and ammunition,
hunted foxes and parrots.

I grew sleepless and made night
my daylight, colouring the sky
with hallucinogens and narcotics,
wandering with agitation.

I watched bullets
fly unspent from the breech,
my brother unloading
as fast as I could load.

And watching over the farm,
I struck a ram in the ute,
and cradling its heavy, horned head,
its broken neck, decided to shoot it dead.

Something shifted, something disconnected,
and I went up to the wheatbins
with a damaged sense of self,
distressed as fellow workers shot cats.

And then backpacking from Bali
to Nepal, other possibilities
mocked and harried my predicament:
the hunger to score, the cliché of searching.

Part of me broke free
in the highest mountains
and settled in a temple tree,
though I didn't know it.

A bus accident and a litany
of death – a chopper in to take
away the wounded, corpses
left broken at the bottom of ravines.

To return without having really left,
to drink and drug to oblivion –
without art, without creativity –
just damage and loss and death.

To move into the squat
in Fremantle, where vegetables
were the only food when there was food,
to sign away from meat in self-disgust.

To retreat south with my brother
and girlfriend, to climb the flooded gum
on the roadside beside the dairy,
where tired cows dragged tonnes of hoodwink.

To wake one morning in asbestos walls,
the spring cold leaching in from irrigated fields,
swollen jerseys calling into the fog
to be relieved of their burdens.

To talk it out over breakfast,
dollops of cream the body and blood.
Haycarting we'd been told
the 'old girls' would make blood and bone.

To take wing and flit north
then south again, into the settler's chestnut tree,
looking down at the haters
poisoning water, driving us out.

Living in a field of cattle
earmarked for slaughter – young
'Molly B12' nuzzling our hands,
the screaming fox at night.

I was vegan and returned
to my girlfriend alone in the shack.
My brother had found his own way
and I sang my song of living flesh.

A decade of flying, staying
above ground while every fibre
yearned for obliteration, held together
by an ethics of Pythagoras.

In rehab, living in the Globe Hotel
or the Supreme Court Gardens,
hearing of friend after friend
dying of overdose, the song

kept me alive. Shivering
by the sea, colder inland
on a star-blown night I listened
to animal-sounds secure.

And when I joined forces
with the woman who knew
the same – one who had abandoned
habits of flesh-eating years before,

I vanished into the Indian Ocean,
went crazy on a coral speck eating
coconuts and rice, shreds of green and chilli
from the islands' greenhouses.

To break the cycle. Break free.
Rejoin the animal world, the kingdom
without hierarchy. But still sleepless,
some call me crazy, edgy.

I renounce all organised religion
and feel liberated spiritually,
no animals are slaughtered
to pave my way to plenty.

Plenty is sharing space,
Plenty is hearing another's breath,
Plenty is every atom of the biosphere,
Plenty is the weapon that cannot hurt me.

Returning home the other day,
we discovered a spatterwork of blood
by the front door, and only today
after noticing a lone doe with joey do I see.

The mob broken up in our absence
by gunfire, the doe sheltering by the house,
our shelter – this is more than Heidegger
could make of dwelling to Celan in the forest.

Refuge is the key. Refuge is where
no creature will be killed by us for flesh
but will make its own way – fences down
and passage no *rite de passage* condescended by us.

Almost three decades have passed.
I have learnt not to proselytise, and this
song is not a commandment. My song
is still a lament, and I perch high

in the old York gum that lost a limb
in the last storm – I hear the owl
homing in on its prey, and have nothing
to say against its way, knowing it's not my way.

High temperatures are shredding this environment
self-designed over millennia to take the heat –
failsafes have failed and a backup isn't in place.
Fire ran close to us just last night.

My fingers are not claws,
my teeth are not for tearing,
my legs are not for running down,
my feet not for trampling.

The music I hear is not all sweetness –
the abattoir fills my ears with blood,
the paddock with sheep conversations
firebreaks itself with burning flesh.

There's no denying the truth –
the 'sacrifice' of animals to human
addiction and *thanatos*. This omnicultural
worshipping of death to affirm life.

I breathe past the smoke, breathe
in clear blue sky. Though no watercress
to hand, I eat pulses and leafy greens –
the water deep below quivers under our weight.

They say I am mad,
out of my tree, as I eat
fruits and nibble leaves,
harvest nuts and make tempeh.

I listen to the peace
like static around a world at war,
I know the real clichés are
in the consuming of the living and the dead.

SWEENEY'S LAMENT

What I glean through gaps in mountains
What I hear of swan's sweeping wings
What I cherish in the green of watercress –

Nary the stain of emptiness?
Nary the signs of wickedness?
Nary the all-fours grinding of distress?

SWEENEY'S REMEDY FOR BATHOS

Lumbered with responsibility
for the off-beam and preposterous,
Sweeney flew headlong into the breeze,
undoing the high falutin' syntax

as you'd expect him to do –
no gravitas, no inversions
or up-endings of word order,
just common speech and a touch

of craziness – idiosyncrasy – thrown in.
It's what's expected of me, he said –
wings moving with the tremolo of a hummingbird
while looking the raptor to those watching from the ground.

I compose my epiphanies
of nonsense that make grave sense
in my sleep. Perched on the bough
of the sacred tree we know

will be cut down. It's part of the joke.
All music flies out the door
though a tin whistle eats away
like refrain. I don't even *look*

like a bird – not *really* – just a splinter
of the broken mirror that's in everyone's eye,
a man in a tree that calls out to be felled.
It could be protest, but it's not.

I am a natural icon, a hero
of language recuperation, the loss
in translation loss, Hölderlin's translations
of Sophocles, a religious revival,

a protector of the old ways. Why shouldn't
the turf-cutter or hunter or logger or miner
watch television? There's not a drop of contradiction
in the liquor. What of the laws of drink-flying?

GRAPHOLOGY CHRONOTYPE 3: SWEENEY

for Tony Barry

Had lost interest in landforms
Had lost interest in eavesdropping
    on chiffchaffs and wrens
Had forgotten about holy wells
    and was deaf to the corrosive church bells

However, he had become transfixed by the *Sheela na gig*
on the decrepit castle keep wall

Staring all day into its helix
Naming it 'she' and feeding it
                old red sandstone
                slate
                blackthorn and whitethorn
                slurry
                freshly mown grass
                tufts of bog cotton
                burning furze
                worn tractor tyres
                uncaulked hulls of sailboats
                feathers from ostracised jackdaws
                shrapnel from old wars
                illuminated manuscripts
                rubbish left by the *Star Wars* film crew
he fell into the vacuum
of its indifference.

A visiting Australian yob saw it for what it was: 'You're just
cunt-struck mate… she's gotya by the balls.'

SWEENEY DEPLORES NATIONALISM IN THE HAZY DAYS OF SUMMER

All is suffused with seed and salt
And the sea ruffles the feathers
Of some-of-the-time residents.
They like the going when
The going is good, he thinks.

Nobody can understand a word
Of my song, but what the hell.
This mixture of tongues is no less
Than the interior of old stone.
Keep the streams and rivers

Clear and don't worry about
The words that describe. Let
Them breathe. Let us gather
Around the bog where broken
White goods sink, where herbicides

Form rainbows and prisms
We see future through. Let us
Welcome those from behind
Barbed wire, waiting five years
In limbo – *their blood* blood too.

All is suffused with seed and salt
And the sea ruffles the feathers
Of some-of-the-time residents
And I will barrack for the opposite
Team to myself or play alien sports.

SWEENEY IN THE HAWTHORN TREE CONFUSED BY HIBERNO-AUSTRALIAN-ENGLISH

That's me, Sweeney, in the flowering
hawthorn tree. It's May, and the blossoms
are on time, hurá hurá, who can tell
if it will work these days! I watch you all

walk past for the rest of the year
taking no notice, but the hawthorns
have got your attention now, and you won't
put a step wrong in your tractors.

Heehee! I am cavorting with the birds,
and not just new arrivals basking
in the leafery, but the stalwarts who stay
when leaves give no shelter – just

a bare circuit-board, shorted out
across the country. And in the smelly
loquacity of the antiphonal fly-loving
flowers, I sing tra-la tra-lee, hear me!

Got some news from Australia today –
so many of my kin sailed sea and sky
to get there – heard some news
that the pig-and-roo-shooting

old man – farmer, land developer –
was found guilty of murdering
an environmental officer. Heard
that the defence played the poor

put-upon farmer card, driven to kill
because of thwartings and 'draconian
environmental laws': the farmer and his family
wanted to chop and clear the vegetation

away, leave it as bare as here. Which
trees are the hawthorn trees of there,
which roots shelter the spirit, keep
the others safe? Whose ancestors

sing in the leaves? My kin tell me
to respect the sheoak needles caught
by an easterly, to stay clear of the roots
coopted by the Christmas tree. I believe them.

Heehee, the death and agony
and the slain guardian of the trees.
I water with my tears as the poet said –
whose colony of angels did he see?

You say I am laughing inappropriately?
It's a nervous habit. I hop to the blackthorn
to spike myself into reality. I can't control
your dream. The effect of feathers

and gravity, of travel in a world
contracted to building materials. I hear
you smug as bugs in rugs, as drinkers
at confession, hitching a ride with the church.

Godbless godless godbless godbless –
let the tourists come and walk beneath
the effusion of flowers in my hawthorn tree,
let the grass be cut and the calves be slaughtered,

let the milk run from the dairies, let the speculator
make a killing. Hurá, hurá – I'm the eejit
crossing his wires, stuck in the hedges, the towers
of the hawthorn. Laugh with me. Laugh at me!

Watch May change to June and the May blossoms
turn pink. Nothing is as it seems. No bird sings
the same song twice over. No birds lives in only
one tree. But each tree lost is misery. Ah, a hot day!
    It's a scorcher! A scorcher! Hurá!

SWEENEY SUFFERS AT THE PAWS OF THE OTTER

*Thereafter, at the end of a day and a night, an otter that was in the lake
came to Ronan with the psalter, and neither line nor letter of it was injured.
Ronan gave thanks to God for that miracle, and then cursed Suibhne,
saying: Be it my will, together with the will of the mighty Lord, that even
as he came stark-naked to expel me, may it be thus that he will ever be,
naked, wandering and flying throughout the world; may it be death from
a spear-point that will carry him off. My curse once more on Suibhne...*

RONAN

7. He seized my psalter in his hand,
    he cast it into the full lake,
    Christ brought it to me without a blemish,
    so that no worse was the psalter.

8. A day and a night in the full lake,
    nor was the speckled...white [book] the worse;
    through the will of God's Son
    an otter gave it to me again.

9. As for the psalter that he seized in his hand,
    I bequeath to the race of Colman
    that it will be bad for the race of fair Colman
    the day they shall behold the psalter.

from *Buile Suibhne*, translated by J. G. O'Keeffe

As if redemption can be thrown into the sea
that taunts this coast of wrecks, even snug
in the semi-rough of Otter Point, the psalter
leaks words into the harbour, the leisure

craft bobbing high to keep up the spirits.
The wind is right to hear the church bell
toll the fatal rocks, as I search for your
surfacing, making shallows deep

with your address to another medium,
superstitious but able to confront the inky
spirits, the anger of nets and lines, sharp
as the catch-and-tear, as I search for your

surfacing, a mouth full of sleek words
and death, my end in the song I sing
from your cataclysm. Already I can sense
rocks and weed vanishing as I grow wings,

higher and higher over, a gull shitting
as you bask on a rock, or let bog-water
spilling from the hills shower you clean,
mingle with antiseptic salt. That book

I wrote! – copying down the talk
of prophets and tyrants – will
always come back to haunt me.
I know, I know, And yet you

make it so easy for them –
sliding up out of calm waters,
handing it to the bastard
      on a plate.

SWEENEY'S FLIGHT OF EXILE

Sweeney flew so far off course
he realised he was willing the error.
He flew over Europe and Africa
then deviated across Madagascar.

La Réunion (le Piton des Neiges was smoking)
to the Cocos-Keeling Islands (a red-tailed
tropic bird distracted him for a day)
onto the coast of Western Australia.

Weary with half a world behind him,
salt in his eyes, he continued inland
until he grew dizzy over vast spreads
of florescent wheat, becoming even

more disorientated than he had
over the limitless oceans, where he'd
found himself uttering shouts frighteningly
close to prayers before the winds shredded them,

threw them back into his face to become
contrails seen by solo yachtsters.
The wheat filled him with grief for the scarce
pickings of his war-torn homeland, for his

own burnings and pillagings and emptying
of silos. And here were vast-roofed
houses and capped cylinders he instinctively
knew were where the fat lobes of wheat would reside

before dispersal among the people. Where
were the people? He joined the butcher bird
in its tearing young red-capped robin chicks
from their nest and said, Lord I know not!

He flew with crazed, ranting parrots
who pecked at spilt grain and were flattened
by beastly war machines. 'Trucks!' they
squawked in their death throes. Inside – in the trucks –

were the elusive people. And the grimaces
on those 'warrior' faces were more indifferent
than those of all the fighters he had dragged into battle.
Sulking in a churchyard Sweeney saw a holy man

watering the dry, plantless ground with an aspergillum.
Sweeney felt he had found a home that could never
be his for the taking. He sat in a defunct tree
and the priest shrieked, 'Leave!' Sweeney

flew high and then plunged burning
into the still-green wheat. A lightning strike
that lit up the incombustible, took out every weed –
Sweeney – trial, biosecurity, a new wave herbicide.

A CHARRED SWEENEY ARISES, BRAINWASHED BY THE STATE, TO IMPRINT HIMSELF ON THE LOCALS TAKING UP THEIR RACIST DESIRES

Betting his myth would work
in this new setting, he alluded
to the narrative of his flight.
It cut no cloth, gained no ground,

got him no favours in this *new* land.
But they taught him the way
of firearms, and soon he was counted
among their hunting parties – gun,

survey map, and beer in hand.
He quickly got the hang of it
and trashed all myths as unscientific.
He became assistant to an anthropologist.

Later, pursuing the mystery of colonial
popularity he worked as a medic
denying bush medicine, and as a trooper
dishing out whiteman's legalities.

Still charred, he whited-up
with the lime they hacked out
and spread over paddocks – the cleared
ground prepped for ASW and hard wheat –

and threw his lot in with the 'whites
only' party (they didn't quite advertise
themselves as such and boasted 'non-whites'
in their ranks), and pulled plenty of votes.

He promised the reinstatement of Terra Nullius.
He promised integration. He promised the right
to bear arms. But then his burnt wings resprouted
on the eve of his political ascension and he rose

into the political glare too fast, to be carried away
south – beyond the sheep-edged continent.
He forgot himself. He became the sun
and fell down into the melting white

of Antarctica. He tried to scratch
his name and his story into the shocking
white of dead water, bring it to life
but he was lost, lost in the white-out.

IS IT HUBRIS WITH WHICH SWEENEY AWAITS THE APPROACH OF A DOUBLE FRONT?

The trail bikes run around endlessly in his head. Revs
gut-wrenching and replete with false lulls. So much
deadwood cleared for the mower to run through,
he incorporates. Nothing to do with business,
but it *is* adjustment. He knows two fronts – bang, bang –

are due to roll over the coastal plain and up into the hill
tonight, tomorrow night. Supplies have been 'got in'
and necessary precautions taken. The ecumenical chapel
in a cottage at Katrine had been washed away by the river's
flexings. A stone causeway built by convicts resisted.

Sweeney was mulling all of this over as the trail bikes
blazed. Winter ignitions. The fury of burgeoning wild oats.
The fronts wired ahead. Summer coming will be furious.
More than chances are. Do I have the depth of character,
the interconnectedness with being and quintessence to cope?

No hope. Buzz slur buzz slur. Confronted. Lulled. Confronted.
Stone by stone, Saint Saviour's rose to exclude the extracurricular.
The graveyard welcomed its guests. Local stone. Displaced
roots of Christmas trees, the inclinations of soil and stone
to move as rains rushed down. It's hubris to map, to report.

SWEENEY – 'LITTLE BIRDIE FLYING HIGH' – SHITS ON A GATHERING OF CRYPTO-FASCISTS BUT MEANS NOTHING AGGRESSIVE BY IT

A natural bodily function. Uplifted and moving
you don't always think over where it will land. End up.
They *were* making a hell of a racket – startling.

Nervous energy. Reaction. No way was *he* ordering
one of those DNA kits to ascertain what percentage
of his feathers were woven on which parcel of land.

Fist shakings are salutes? It was like the 1936
Berlin Olympics. Or the Nuremberg Rallies. If Sweeney
was crass for saying it – out of touch with the zeitgeist –

then he would likely be damned for mentioning the New Guard
or the Fascist Legion or the ribbon cutting on Sydney
Harbour Bridge. It wasn't a big shit he'd dropped,

but it was obviously pungent – Aussie flag bandannas
were now covering eyes as well as noses and mouths.
They are veiling themselves, sang Sweeney, wistfully,
as his shit incited the patriots to fight among themselves.

THE TENETS OR TENANTS OF SWEENEY
for MH

And so… to rouse a whip, coral or corral or currach
like coracle branded hide singed hair no modifier
no not really to live by said decisive Akubra mirage

weaving tufts caught by spinifex bluebush bash-
grab influence as testament of flaying, clothes-hanger
slaughter-hook made allowances for under the Act.

Tenancy is much more than tendency, to round
up a leisurely quote, a jerk of conscience wavering
towards some other matter, a duty, a flippancy, a soak.

And so… farmer, occupant, dishes out the what's what,
signature chastisement as boy mimics father remade
in bush fire-brigade imagery. Burnings. Roo-shoot spotlight.

Cyclops. Down in the valley they rove. Such holdings.
Little give-aways. Persona of compass, here's a navigator.

SWEENEY – BIRD BRAIN DISSEMBLER

Sweeney can't abdicate because he's renounced kingdoms
and property and borders. His old mates call him 'bird brain'.

He hovers, just hovers. He's lost the art of aerial transversal.
He exercised his Irish right of residence in Britannia

to vote 'remain'. The racists tarred and feathered him.
He has feathers on his feathers. It was like the Blitz

Knightclub. White feathers of cowardice. He hovered over
the bigots manning their barricades. (The long lines of refugees

manifesting in their dream narratives.) 'Economic!' they cried.
In Australia, where he co-existed in his bird brain at least,

he heard a Pommy migrant at Hillarys Harbour say that she
exercised her right to vote at a distance: 'Keep migrants out –

Britain for the British.' She missed the irony because Australia
has shifted the grounds of tragedy, made such ironies *faits
accomplis*.

SWEENEY THE THESAURUS BIRD

Sweeney the thesaurus bird doesn't want to be scribed
into any monk's poem. A telling of his doings – no, more

than this: it's as if they know him. So many spatial
and temporal issues it's not worth unfurling feathers.

The yellow or green belly of the ringneck parrot,
one or the other outside its range: him or another?

But he did alight as a pronoun on the whipping branches
of a jam tree that had been killed but still looked sprightly.

Death doesn't creep up; rather, life doesn't arrive
as it once did. The bark-strippers had been to the picnic

spots to strip from head to toe, the leaves laughing
nervously, affect inappropriate. He knows the killers

to be strung out, off their faces, hanging, ripped, blown
away, smashed, blotto, fucked-up, desperate. Greedy.

To take the bark and make a tea, distil it to the essence
of leaf-shaped clouds, green sky and blue ground. Trippy.

DMT – dimethyltryptamine – extracted from the hallowed
tree, short-lived tree revered for the flour its seeds provide.

The parrot's belly is a hallucination. There is no red ridge
over its beak. It's hard to pick whether it's male or female.

The picnic is defamiliarised and the words for *replete*
and *lack* are caught up in the brocade of antonyms

and synonyms. Who's watching the thieves? Dead
perches are disconnection from the earth which speaks

through a taut wire and two tin cans, vibrations
along the line. It's hard to weave a nest

when there are no eggs to be laid. He says this.
Or the druggies say it. It's on the breeze,

that's for sure – going nowhere,
out of whack with its fate.

SWEENEY ENCOUNTERS A RUSSIAN ADVENTURER IN THE AVON VALLEY

Sweeney had to do his shopping at Northam Coles.
There was a lot of kerfuffle in the town and more
than a few foreign voices. He was surprised

to find the foreigners were not being attacked
by locals. On his asking why, a teenager stacking shelves
told him, It's because they'll only be here for a while.

What was going on? Sweeney took to the airwaves.
Birds of a feather, we might interpolate. Just outside town
he came across a vast balloon being spread out and filled with night.

He swooped down and found a man who looked like
a heavily bearded Dennis Hopper. He caught the name
of this wild man whom he recognised as a holy obsessive.

Almost like me, he said. A Russian. There were many voices
speaking Russian. I know Russian, said Sweeney – I get pictures
wired to my headspace from a poet in his country *dacha*

every winter, every summer. It's cold here in winter,
but not as cold as it gets in Russia. That's the definition of cold
in overheated times. The balloon was filling and the zeal

of the adventurer was palpable. All of this just for him.
His name was Fedor Konyukhov. He was aiming to loop
the earth from sunrise. To smash a record. The media, cloying
    and clinging,

were saying he sees the world as a place to conquer: mountains,
oceans, everything. Sweeney could see vast swathes of mangroves
dying in the far side of the country but in his gondola Fedor
    Konyukhov

would fly nowhere near them. Sweeney watched the balloon rise
with the sun, hung around and did a couple of interviews,
     then flew back
to Coles to finish his shopping. I feel like the stork delivering
     my own birth,
he said, adding a few more cans to his stash.

SWEENEY DEPLORES THE RISE OF THE FASCISTS

i.m. Niall Lucy on what would have been his 60th

Time was never out of joint, mate, a hermit on the plain
above Madura Pass tells Sweeney. And those who think so
just want the text of the earth to be read in a different way.

And so the spectres of eagles killed on the great highway
ranging east to west and back again, eagles killed pulling
at the sinew and fur of kangaroos *roadkilled* in their thousands,

eagles killed plucking plumes from emu carcasses, caught
out by the bullbars of semi-trailers ploughing through the expanse
as dawn snaps and the blue-bush spark to life in the dry air.

Listen, says the hermit, Hear the vanishing call of the vanishing
quail-thrush, hear the dogger's vehicle come back from his
        killings,
hear the deceased dingos calling the moon down to the treeless

horizon. You are haunted, the hermit says, You are haunted
by the toxins falling from the mouths of demagogues – angry
whites who cherish the idea of DNA, swilling from chalices

of pure hate, rallying around their flags gifted to them by
        the warfare
of their ancestors. You are haunted by the chiasmus of the pass
rising and falling – plain to plain – at sunset, the Major Mitchells

coming in to find a stand of trees on the burning edge, bound down
by the renaming they've had imposed on their own language,
and on the language of those they've co-existed with for so
        very long.

And looking out / into the openness of the waterless place,
where *not* walking doesn't mean the non-presence of ghosts,
the hermit says, It doesn't mean...! And Sweeney identifies.

We are one and the same, they say, as the patriots taste
their foul air and make God do their dirty work and deliver
themselves unto. These are the scriptures of *every other*

making, making their bloody points. Sweeney swivels over
the karst and wonders where he will land once he sets forth?
Which tower can I alight on without burning up?
Who will share my ancient songs?

SWEENEY TRIES TO WARN LOCALS OF THE DANGER
OF A RADIOACTIVE WASTE DUMP

They live in a ghostworld and don't realise they'll die into
    reality.
These retired admirals and governors, these captains of
    industry,
these workers who feel they've liberty and will get the trickle-
    down.

And they will. The seepage, the extramural, the dull sheen
    of haunted
eyes, the creeping pallor, the cancers that can't be fixed to
    one time
or one place, or other. I worry how serious I've become away

from my myth, that parable from which all other crazy tales
spin out. In a lone tree in the place they call a waste of space –
just kangaroos and emus, bluebush and the cattle they haul

from pillar to post. Fact is, those creatures aren't ghosts,
    they're flesh
and blood and this is their life. Their souls here and now.
    Cradle to grave.
And so the antinomians know the common good is measured
    by the feeling,

the sense that it's their good. This is all I can extract from
    their festivals
of the arts, their entertainments, versions of Harlequin and
    Columbine on
wide, colonial streets. Patches of land at Maralinga cleaned
    up of plutonium,

returned to traditional owners. I hover over Barndioota, and
     know a right-
wing ex-senator is showing his wisdom and largesse, and
     the purpose-built
Mammon is where his over-accumulation will be trans-
     formed, where life

and death will do good business, where ghosts will come to
     life. I have
lost my spark, the wit of the village idiot. Down in Adelaide
     they talk
defence contracts and big money, and submarines made from
     local steel.

I speak out, yell stock epithets at them, say there is no beauty
     to behold.
Birds I can't recognise tell me I'm just a human with feathers.
But all the world will know us, they say. All they are will
     end up here.
And I, shot down in flames, burn out of their stories.

SWEENEY GOES TO SING 'ALL THINGS BRIGHT AND BEAUTIFUL' BUT NO SOUND ISSUES FORTH

No place to perch. Each great tree falling to the bloody-
     minded,
the selfish, the silly. So many trees out there, one fella says,
as one of the twelve remaining 'Jarrah Kings' of the Swan
Coastal Plain crashes into wetlands. No place to perch
high enough to sing out, no place to perch old enough
to cope with the implication of a prehensile nature.
I am migratory, he says, I will sing and leave.
I am no threat. And the cutwood bitter taste
makes his syrinx muddy with parataxis.
This is not innovation, this is not resistance,
he admits, dry-throated. So rising high
and crossing the Scarp, he detects tall trees
in the town of Northam on the restively named
Avon River. Name seems a bit out of place,
he thinks, but I will find a stage, a place to sing
from. But as he hovers about its crown, the great tree
wavers and a cracking, a splintering, rises like revelation
up through its aerial body, sparking across to Sweeney.
And then it falls. Or rather, it is lopped chunk by chunk
down to the base – a 'safe' removal. All I want is a place
to sing 'All Things Bright and Beautiful', he laments.
I am ready to embrace their God. I am ready to meet
them halfway. I have such a voice to lend if only
they'd let me connect, if only they'd tune in.

SWEENEY CONTEMPLATES A DISPLAY OF FORCE
BY THE POLICE STATE

Distant now, and working out how to make a return, how
　　to embrace
the wetlands and detrack the machines, Sweeney flew low
　　through the rain
of grasshoppers rising up from the denuded plains, late crops
　　shaking
their seed onto the scorched earth. I will return to the coastal
　　plain,

said Sweeney loud to the parrots, loud to the crows, loud to
　　the mulga
snakes, loud to the grasshoppers. I will stand with the
　　protectors against
the troops of the dictator, against the builder of stadia and
　　his wealthy,
uncouth mates. I will stand against their class pretensions,
　　against their

sporting codes which read a little like the bishop leading an army
against the heathen. I *am* a heathen, Sweeney told the blue sky
stretched to breaking point; I am old as the earth but can't
　　even perch
on the outstretched branch of a York gum without feeling
　　guilt. But I will fly

down to the marri, to the blackbutt, to the banksia, to the
　　zamias and grass
trees and ask if I might perch temporarily, temporarily to
　　watch over
the souls of those who dwell there, who know the stories,
　　who connect

constellations with earth itself, who can unpick the codes,
the fever

of growth, schematics of belonging. Red-tailed black cockatoos
will guide me in, give me strength. I will ask to join the lines,
speaking
my ancient tongue of respect. I will tell the police they must
listen
to the ground through their feet, must listen to the whispering

coming out of the bush where there are as many worlds
as night reveals, spreading its sheet, a future unfurled.

SWEENEY INSIDE THE WOUND, THE GRAVEYARD, THE DEATHZONE

Accompanying the red-tailed black cockatoos,
Sweeney wavered in the brittle air and plummeted
deep into the wound, the graveyard, the deathzone.

Gasping, he knew immediately that he'd be violently ill,
that The One who had been going *to & fro, up & down*
across the damaged earth, would smite him also,

mark him with the indelible blood of the wound.
The mountain of uprooted grass trees, their name – *balga* –
resonating through future epochs of pitch and sulphur,

and marri trees that won't ever blossom again,
the torn capillaries and veins of time, all wondering
if they be dead or undead, sap retreating with syntax,

photosynthesis in slow shutdown. Sweeney spoke
loud to the man-becoming-cockatoo – James – to whom
the policeman had said, 'Get away or I will kneecap you',

who beheld the betrayers and documented The Fall –
cockatoo with clipped wings, disorientated inside
the wound the graveyard the deathzone.

SWEENEY THE BARN OWL OPENS HIS EYES WIDE IN BROAD DAYLIGHT

Sweeney looks down at the people coming out of the hospital –
they have seen him, he knows it in his bones. Yes, now their eyes
search his eyes and the shock of light reaches as far inside

as the flames that drove him out of the tall tree on the hillside.
Where can I rest? he asks them. The Main Roads are cutting
  down
all the old-growth wandoos and salmon gums and York gums,

slicing through their anniversaries with a righteousness
that will truck no argument. These living heritage buildings
we conduct our lives in and around, *our* places of eating and
  worship.

Sweeney shuts his eyes on them, high up in the gum that clings
to the edge of the car-park. Tonight he will fly south-east,
  aiming
to reach the great trees still remaining on the York-Quairading

Road before they are brought down, before red-tailed
  phascogale
and Carnaby's black cockatoo and rainbow bee-eater are forced
to find somewhere else to feed and nest and hide from owl,
  or *vanish* –

and in the matutinal revelation that abbreviates his waking
  hours,
upside down in a tree-killer's world, Sweeney will hoot at
  their stupidity,
a klaxon-call just before the crash that will wipe us all out.

SWEENEY'S LAST WILL AND TESTAMENT

He woke to find he was turning back into a human.
This horrified him more than the nightmare that had
jerked him awake – that the singing honeyeaters

were calling out to him, singing loud, to save them
as the bulldozer blade wiped out their habitat. And above
the controls of the machine were massive white faces,

whiter than all the heritage of Europe, grinning
white faces of South Park artwork, with speech bubbles
emitting in slow farts of, 'We can clear whatever

we want now… so fuck you chardonnay socialists,
fuck you city dwellers, fuck you tree-huggers, fuck
you who don't know a thing about farming, fuck

you who don't understand that we have our *kulchur*,
too!'. And Sweeney, awake and watching his brilliant
if bedraggled plumage corroding, saw his skin beneath

was numinous or luminous – the metaphors
collapsing into the myth – *white*, and choked
on his owl pellet of self-awareness. Where

can I go now? he asked. They are okay with my
having killed holiness, they are okay with my
having been a war-mongering vengeance-seeking royal.

If I smile back they'll accept me into their sheepfold.
If I do business with them they'll celebrate my epiphany.
If I turn a blind eye. If I let the singing honeyeaters perish.

He woke to find he was turning back into a human.
He pleaded for sleep to return him to the site of destruction.
I will become one with the honeyeaters. I will die.

54

SWEENEY WITNESSES THE ATTACK ON THE COOLBELLUP BUSH BY THE FORCES OF A CORRUPT POLICE STATE

for Tahlia and Emma

Wings clipped, you'd expect Sweeney to plunge
to the ground, plough into the ploughed sand
and wait helpless till collected by the mulcher
and spat into a pile of has-beens, signed-off on.

Wings clipped, you'd expect Sweeney to plunge
into the clouds of toxic dust generated by the smash-
and-grab, by the sweeping of the last pieces
from the board in an endgame not quite going to plan.

Wings clipped, you'd expect Sweeney to plunge
into the microclimate of asbestos, the bush stressed
as dumping ground for waste no one wants to pay for,
then murdered because other forms of life test reality's limits.

Wings clipped, you'd expect Sweeney to plunge
into the crowd of protesters, some wearing face masks,
others exposed to the dust that reaches into front gardens,
houses, the small amount of space allotted to public recreation.

Wings clipped, you'd expect Sweeney to plunge
into the police lines, police told to watch out for the particles,
that it will cost them too in the long run, but the Big Cop
says hold your positions, breathe in, breathe out, it's all
    propaganda.

Wings clipped, you'd expect Sweeney to plunge
into the bulldozer, stuff up its hydraulics, its bamboozled
driver bragging of his agency. And all the while the women
up the trees looking down and roosting, roosting, roosting.

55

Wings clipped he lifted, flying high, to sit close with Tahlia.
Wings clipped he lifted, flying high, to sit close to Emma.
Together, he said, Together we will keep the trees upright.
Together, he said, We will unravel the bulldozer, the mulcher.

HAVING GIVEN UP THE GHOST, SWEENEY FLIES IN WITH SEEDLINGS TO HELP STITCH THE WOUND

A traumatic wound – gashed open to the bone.
But the Emperor and his Jester are up the creek
without a paddle, wading against their own effluent.

A traumatic wound – gashed open to the bone.
The spell feeding on the workers like dermonecrosis
is broken, and they disperse into healthier skin.

A traumatic wound – gashed open to the bone.
Having given up the ghost, Sweeney flies in with
seedlings of native vegetation to help stitch the wound.

A traumatic wound – gashed open to the bone.
In the sand the bushland had grown from, Sweeney
knows country is still alive and consults with the Elders.

A traumatic wound – gashed open to the bone.
It can be healed. Its essence is spilling out like a balm.
The red-tailed cockatoos are thinking of the decades ahead.

SWEENEY DREAMS HE'S HAVING A NIGHTMARE
OF CLEARING

In his dream Sweeney sees himself de-feathered and crashed
　　in the grey sand,
unable to pull himself out of sleep, locked into a nightmare
　　of a bulldozer
running across the land like an electric razor, the entire bush
　　falling
to its gigantic all-encompassing blade. Nothing stops it, not even
the largest jarrah and marri trees, nothing just nothing will thwart
its progress, not even boulders setting their shoulders against
the onslaught. Sweeney in his dream tries to stop the nightmare
in its tracks, and calls on those who have become his friends
　　to help him:
Forgive me for my mis-sayings for my well-meant efforts that
　　have failed.
Forgive me for not spreading my wings wide enough to
　　protect you all.
And with that he rises from the sand and squawks so loud
　　the driver
halts his deadly machine, and leaps down and jabs his finger
into Sweeney's charred breast, like an image out of a painting
yet to be painted, and says, Now listen, buster, this is how I make
my living, and who are you to take food from my table?! And
　　Sweeney,
feeling the sway of his argument and feeling himself fall back
into the nightmare, sees his own beak moving, hears his own
　　words
tumble past the nub of his tongue in more than mimicry of
　　a human voice:
But when it's all gone, you'll have no more work anyway and
　　the world
will be dying. And the bulldozer driver replies, You may be right,
but what would you have me do? — this is my job, and I

know no other.

And with this Sweeney wakes, from both dream and night-
mare and sweating

and feeling for his feathers to find them black and red and
white and intact,

and says: I will fly high and watch over them all, I will fly
from grey sand

over gravel and ochre loam and granite and brown clay. And
in doing so

he flies past Walwalinj which the colonisers call Mount Bakewell,

and watches the fires the farmers have lit to eat their stubble
and chaff

from the last harvest running over their firebreaks into the
shreds of bush

remaining from past clearings and past *burnings-off*, and he
watches a digger

knocking down four magnificent York gums – ancient solar
systems

of life – to make a paddock even more vacant, more productive

in the short term, but dead to the future, and he cries and cries

but his tears put out neither the fires nor the work-zeal of the
clearer

doing a job as night falls, and the kangaroo's head is renamed

the Southern Cross and the ends of the earth play

on the stereos of machinery and cars and houses

and personal devices. Sweeney

in his dream of a nightmare.

INTERLUDE

THE OLD PROFESSORS TRY TO KNOCK SWEENEY OFF HIS PERCH IN THE HÖLDERLINTURM

Sweeney flutters in through the open window,
flutters in over the twilit river with its punts
propelled by the hands of drunk students

shouting in time, shouting in time with the coxswain,
shouting in time with the punter, gambolling
on the once numinous waters of the Neckar.

Sweeney flutters in through the open window,
over the head of the German professors, *experts*
on the poet whose shrine they inhabit,

flutters in and drops a version of 'Hälfte des Lebens'
in an enemy language, a language as inarticulate
as struggle for voice in the poem, the swans mute

with their land-in-water occupancy suddenly full of voice
somewhere out there in the haze of a summer
eve, somewhere on the verge of the death

of culture, as if their wings had come loose
with fruit dropping into the silty water, into
the pollution that has nothing to do with Dionysius,

with the hope for a better world. And Sweeney,
now on his perch, is batted down with a hand in disgust,
this travesty of a bird that thinks it's sane

and hasn't yet been to the precise sources of the Neckar,
to the ancient ways that lead all flightpaths
to the one explosion of language, grit of research.

Sweeney flutters against the window
which has now been closed, flutters with his
fantasias and off-beat wing-beats, flutters

until he drops feathers which are brushed
aside, as no offerings of peace are acceptable,
and the life of the icon will be as it has always

been, revealed by each thesis, each venturing
into fact. And out there, out where Sweeney
should be, the swan-song is at a critical stage
    before darkness shakes the panes.

BOOK TWO
After Hölderlin

AFTER 'FRIEDENSFEIER' [CELEBRATION OF PEACE]

*It's out of my hands, but here is a sample. All those words dressed
up as song filling my ears from the denuded fringes of city.*

    A woodchipper is eating the cut branches
and cut trunks of trees deemed unnecessary –
it's been going on for weeks – and the grinding-
chewing effect is an affect without a single note
of sweetness, and now a chainsaw – no getting
away from them in any of the treed places
of the world, and the hills cushion the hacking
reverberation, force it through their syrinxes.
It's all collusion from municipal elsewheres,
from civic buildings in the old town,
the zigzag of ancient wood mimicry,
as nightfall approaches and those
last organics are spat into the receptacle.

    But I have my eyes and ears peeled,
listening beyond the deathsounds, waiting
to catch the late-early calls of the riverbird.
It sticks around through winter, making
the best of what's on offer. Generations
of conflict along these narrow banks,
the poisoned grasses, the long-gone
common reeds. But I am standing
in for you in this celebration of peace
talks – the connivings of Munich
to let death stop in Syria, a bit.
God has decided on unity.
A shell burst antiphony.

    But I am not the protagonist of this text.
That is you. And when I say I, I mean you.

It's about the space we occupy and what is claimed.
How much is apportioned to the bargaining table.
Which fragment of us will fit where. Oriental.
Occidental. What is a 'country' where well over
ten percent of the population has been eliminated?
Strain to hear the glorious Muwashshah through the AK47
death rattle, the artillery barrages. Which feast day
are we celebrating? What dangles from the gunbelt?
What corruption of the sacral, of the rhyme
that plays on eternity, the irrelevance of time,
the beat of the darabukkah embracing the sublime
strains of oud and quanun. What of these flowers
in the spiritual garden, the banquet hall
of old men and old women and the young
who accompany them? What of them all? What of Aleppo?

We would invite you over but the water
is so deep, is so wide, is so measured by the weight
of coin fallen through its bloody nets over millennia.
That Syrian palm. Elusive shade. The testy winter sun.
As the monuments fall to the bloody-minded, the clouds
refuse to carry you anywhere. Flight. And now to fight
'people smugglers' they have their NATO warcrafters
patrolling to benefit us all. In the wild places
of European cities, where the balance of nature
is so delicate. Deadly as the shadows of houses on houses,
on the historic tourist places we celebrate. Heaven
sends its boats. You can all be on them.

All this fire. Bricks and mortar and metal
and flesh burn easily. These otherworld attacks,
right out from the rim of a Philip K Dick replicant
solar system. Those lively banters in the drone
HQ. Smart phones that find their way

into any wartorn store. Effective distribution.
Demand supply is demanded. A music of joyousness,
the timbre of the praying human voice.
It chooses to pray. It is not compelled.
To drift over the ocean floor,
to bob in the waves, to driftwood
the beaches. Remember, 'movement
of the people'! We have forgotten about
them all, and forget ourselves as we move
further in. Or fly over, wanting the kinder sun.

So we're asked to stop what we're doing
and do it another way. Who is doing the asking?
Silence works the conventions of language. It's a mask.
Each word added to the lexicon, dragged
into the pop-cultural whirlpool. Where can we hide
in the sensorium? We find ourselves out, the multiplication
of images weighing down the memory banks of world.
Red kite, barbary falcon, Syrian ostrich, little grebe, pharaoh
    eagle-owl; goldcrest.
From this point to that. All the way up to the levelling-off.

    Don't underestimate the amount of time spent
wondering how much of creation a single Hypecoum
    grandiflorum (Papaveraceae)
occupies. The contemplation that has no news conference, that will not
prove Einstein right (always right), that will not challenge the gasp
of a black hole, the weight of the sun that draws it out of itself,
makes grow. In the stench of body decay, the stench
of explosives, the stench of testosterone mirroring megalomania,
the human condition mutates. Even on feast-days, someone
is out of kilter, someone is on a different timetable.
Bomb first, party later. And so held is all dominion.
This proof sheet. Negative when negatives

aren't to be found blown hot in the rubble, washed in the sea.
  Old ways.

  Hymns and thunderstorms. Cloud-seeding.
Autobiographies of weather. Borders selectively porous.
We the blessed, we the cherished, we the children of,
stunted. Gather the flock. Wash the feet.
Eat delicacies after the hot sun has set,
a dusting of snow not far south of Munich.
And mountains, ominous mountains, nearby.
And so immortality is handed out,
doled out, ladled and deposited and secured.
The house is open the house is full
the house is bombed by those who made it.
It tests language, historical knowledge, loyalty,
then implodes. The fumes off the river.
A child playing on a hand-me-down bike.
A washing machine. Bright cheeks. Living.

  Those breezes. We know where we are, don't I.
I, we, tasting our surroundings. Where we too
first steps. Gone. Arms manufacturers,
the makers of computers and software.
And God too, with children.
The oldest mother who
hasn't seen this all. Behind
the walls of her home,
watching the finances.
hoping to make ends meet.
Veils of light if you like.
Withheld is not restrained.
And those who would need power
to answer their fall, their loss. The song of earth
long-gone for them. Call it back. Kill none.

We enjoy the sweet fruits
of dry, hot places. The palms
and aqueducts, the lighthouse minarets,
the reach into affirmation of God. Bright fruit
and bright birds and intricate patterns
that aren't wealth but being, the will of the heavens.
Those intricate weapons that fall
brutally down, rough with cruelty.
Artisan dystopia. The weapons factory
in Vermont, or the Urals, or among the vines
of France, or entwined in the rail or road network
of Britain, or the bomb-makers' arrogant hands
steady in a mud hut, gloating over the constraints,
deftness with limited 'tools'. Never heaven's shape.

The foundations will be the bodies
of children. Under new buildings. Rebuild.
Not even bones left to count. The lion
has retreated, and is eaten out of house
and home. The eternal royal hunt,
with courtiers coming from their
own disaffection, their own failure
of choice, their sons swinging
the sword they themselves
had used to hack their way
out of the womb. Forgive them.
Raise them to the light. Let them
fester and ripen and sweeten under the harsh rays
of an overly familiar sun, let them warm with the rest of us,
leave no one behind. But most, such vast numbers of most,
are glorious and living with a knowledge
of harmony and hope and sharing and light
and we can never close them out. Us out.
You and I. We are here for us all. Then rest.

FLAMES AFTER HÖLDERLIN: WENN ÜBER DEM WEINBERG [WHEN ABOVE THE VINEYARD]

When flames curl over the vineyard
And a coal-fired wind
Blackens the breathless hills,
The colonial vineyard
Just beyond town is a late summer
Sentinel; grapes not set and bursting like fat cells;
Fire wicking the vines as volunteers
Fight off the harvest, notes of aroma.

BARELY HÖLDERLIN'S 'VOM ABGRUND NEMLICH'
[FROM THE ABYSS IN FACT]

It's a gap we cross
every day as we wake.
And we're not alone in this.
Our offspring. A son who,
when small, feared lions and tigers
would cross the Indian Ocean,
stalk through the York gum woodlands,
replace sunrise with bared teeth.
We made this
from our sensuousness
in a Sears house on the edge
of a wood where deer
hid in the shadows of black walnut, town dogs barking mad.
Surely there is no *dog* in me, though I feel empathy
with their drive to find what
they want. When I walk country roads
and bush tracks and between hedges
of fuchsias near Schull, the Shaper
of all patterns
tampers with my
human template. There's nothing
I'd specifically call *my* garden, though I generally tend,
and watch over. From inland
to the coast, I hear sharp winds
rouse the pits and hollows,
reshape rock before me.
New crops are set outside Tübingen.
In early. Green carpets of barley and legumes.
Officials are cutting down and rooting out
trees that don't comply. I am learning
things against desire – but
I find no strength in avoidance.
My senses are fragmented, dispersed

over continents. I am grateful
for the slippage of eucalypt
into lemon into pine resin.
All these gatherings. A politics
forms without nation and I slip
away. Remember
                    our sensuousness. How sunlight
worked the crystal a previous occupant
had hung outside the window

to twist colour, to twist   its way in like seed.

SUBTEXTING 'DER SPAZIERGANG' [THE WALK]

Spray-painted woods
don't welcome the fool
and his crew – the 'Juice Krew'
led by 'Jimbo', jester
in his hat, dragger
of the trolley laden
with beer and paint.
We walk under bare
boughs, and step
into the ploughed
muddy field to let
the fast tractor race
by, and I hold myself
upright clutching a thin
enlichened branch
of a fruit tree near
the murky pond
with its dishevelled
bulrushes. And the fool
and his crew move closer
and closer up the hill,
wrestling and spilling
their beers, girls hauled
into the air, riding
their satyrs. Sleet slices
through the canopy
and the bare forest quivers.

SEARCHING 'DER SPAZIERGANG' [THE WALK]

The woods are closed
till February the eighteenth,
being private woods.
With too much in me,
I want to get between
even the bare trees,
even where there are ixodidae
that spread Lyme disease.
I will be wary, and bare
little skin. I do not want
to attract or disturb ticks.
And it is not 'tick fever season'.
I will have a better chance
in this demi-cold. I'll be out
of the cycle. Freelance.
If I just place one foot carefully
in front of the other and keep
to myself. I will note the well-
tended small gardens and then farmlets
and fields and it will all
come together in a quaint
picaresque. I will not see
the paint spraycans
tossed aside, and graffiti
is the script of some kindly
little god. Powerlines.
They're a thread to follow.
Asbestos roofing fruitful
terrain for moss. Field fringes
have been well herbicided –
winter need not be left
to do all the work. The
Neue Ammer will carry
the stains away. Bliss
under grey or blue skies.

WINTER: ARTIFICIAL LAKE HEADING TOWARDS MELTDOWN

'So glänzet die Natur mit ihrer Pracht auf Erden.' (Thus
nature shines on earth with its bounty.)
FRIEDRICH HÖLDERLIN

It's still frozen, but only just. An interlude.
Food for thought – 'glas' – but reality is a food
Wrapper, a drink container, a spinning football
Hurled onto the phased mirror – experimental.

Water birds have flown the coop. Brow-beaten. Targets.
Already winter's short display of bitterness
Is ending. The melt will let the rubbish sink. Tales
Of crossing into iced worlds generic as sales.

INVERTING 'GEH UNTER, SCHÖNE SONNE'
[GO DOWN, LOVELY SUN]

I'd ask you to reappear from behind the wet blanket, Sun,
   But the ozone has been eaten by refrigerants
      And we can't take your glare. We are people
         Of the skin cancers, tuned by solar flares.

So, whatever your good intentions towards the solar system,
   The galaxy, however far back to the beginning your light
      Reaches, we remain tentative, so easily led by your
         Coming and going, we are trapped in this metaxy.

I have a burnt spot on my macula, a legacy, a result, a consequence:
   Love of gazing into the brightest light, the *solar acetylene,*
      The fiery magnesium ribbon, the deceptions of eclipse.
         On this dark, wintry day I won't ask

That you slough off the cloud, pierce the dark-hearted vapour.
   Nature is outside eyesight and latent growth below the surface
      Still wrestles with absolute darkness. What blessing
         Is bestowed by residues of warmth alone?

HÖLDERLIN'S 'ABENDPHANTASIE' [EVENING FANTASY] AND THE UNWELCOMINGS OF *HERE*

Within the loop the farmlets aren't commercial by order of the Shire.
　　The retired farmer's compulsion is to crop his six acres
　　　　Up to housewalls. A wheat crop he will harvest. His
　　　　　　Tractor spits black fog which falls over all of us.

A visitor rides his bike into the valley – a rare sight. He hears the chug
　　Of the tractor, and shots being fired at a mass of corellas,
　　　　As he struggles up the hill, full of doubts. Where
　　　　　　Else can I ride outside the city? Breaking

Away into the country, to get a taste. Sick to death of concrete,
　　He has smiled at the old colonial houses, the tatty vineyards
　　　　First planted in the nineteenth century, the falling down
　　　　　　Barns. Local colour, he smiles inwardly.

As the evening approaches he must make landfall. He has no lights
　　On his bike. He has left the city to embrace the unknown. Knock
　　　　On a farmhouse door and ask for a bed overnight. He can offer
　　　　　　To pay. He wants wallpaper and evening warmth.

The retired farmer has halted his tractor on the firebreak. He is talking
　　With the cyclist, a stranger. You've gotta be joking! he laughs
　　　　On hearing the request, the sun already set within the halo
　　　　　　Of hills. You better hot foot it back into town

Before it's dark, mate. People around here don't trust this sort of thing.
　　We have a car rally each year but that's different – an excuse
　　　　For a piss up. Then he cocks his head and says to the cyclist,
　　　　　　Aint gotta bottle of something strong in ya backpack?

REACHING INTO 'DES MORGENS' [IN THE MORNING]

The cloudburst has shattered the riverbanks
   And we float unseasonal on high ground.
      Leaves are down in plumes that make no bed
         And locality shakes out its false prophets

Who claim what they don't even know. Even when dry
   Which is the usual state of affairs, you know flow
      Has marked all erosions and the wind's breakers
         Follow the lines of retreat. Which psalter

Opens the trails from camp to camp, which overlays
   Speak across translations to trap outcomes in their time?
      New birds arrive early, to get in while the going is good,
         And hearsay rushes of blood on the high water

Line is a blast of youth in an old country, so old the volcanoes
   Have erupted only in dust, quick as manna wattle sprouting
      And ghosting with projected intense summer heat;
         I would walk the trails! I would take

Happiness to the cleaners and illuminate the firebreaks overgrown
   With greenery that will be summer tinder if not scraped away.
      But live your life and glow under the morning sun –
         Your journey to seed will be left intact.

IN LIEBLICHER BLÄUE? [IN THE GENTLE BLUE]

The sky's blue wallop as a two-hundred-year-old plane tree
Thuds into Neckar Island. He is watching this tactical severing
Through the central window of his tower. The river is flowing
Fast around the altar of Sunday walks and he recalls a once free

And easy sapling rising to bud. He chatters. The tree-bark's sheen
Is beaten metal to the jagged sawteeth which claw its own
Interior, and the upper limbs are steeples, splintered mirrors, reaching
Into. A coal tit whispers freakouts. Four years past two women
    planted candles

Inside a cleft in another island tree, a touchy-feely Valentine's gesture,
And the touchy tree turned into its own chimney, a crown of fire.
He hears blue reverberations and a grey silt of demi-cloud bundles
The old blueness away. In Saxony a crowd cheer as buildings for
    refugees burn,

While youths seriously hinder fire-fighters getting through late winter.
Who knew the bells were ringing silence? He knew and said: I,
    I the abater.

OEDIPUS SPEAKS: AFTER HÖLDERLIN'S *SOPHOCLES'* *OEDIPUS* SECOND ACT SCENE ONE OPENING SPEECH

Earache of your bellyaching
to better the inner illness
in your weightlifting upending
of this quest for weirdness
of visitors and the mess of badness
where I too was citizen now among citizens,
Cadmians, as I might utter to Laius
(and I include Labdacus's offspring
in my call for knowing), I say unto,
let me have the rundown and do
not quiver into the fold of night,
exile into safety, but verily I say
the day of another geography
where business opportunities
will await splendiforously
in my own image, but if not,
and not takes the weight,
as quivering before a significant
other or ego points, a polygraph
declaration of sound waves tapping
the eardrum of (my) self, and let
me know be rebuffed in the choir
of my damnation as I own skyscrapers
and shopping malls and fund a centre
of excellence at the university,
scholarships resonating my name
in the glorious explosions
of the Hammersely Ranges
where no hand washing with scant
water resources will wash away
the guilt of naysayers, of oppositional
home-makers or claimants I know
better than in my paternal wisdom.

And bring out the six-shooters
in Western sunsets to worship
Pytho and pastoral lease
and even a buddy takes on
inclemency to face my resolve
laid bare while he hides in scrubby
domain as if a roof overhead
is anything to crow about; all
this cursing and foul language
enough to block country's ears
to drillcore God's cleanskin
search party, as death is bones
picked clean and white arrangement
under that godforsaken sun. Down
at Cottlesloe Beach I catch waves
of their doubt and play good father
to my progeny and model husband
to the world, which is fated to be smaller
than I am. Father, what do you expect,
legacy of wrestling match, who did over
the Labdacus signature on earth's search
warrant, and the whole Polydorus claim
and the Cadmus sheep nibbling
down to the roots, so sparse,
so judged by the southern switch-aroo,
the plough plodding its boustrephedon
I can read bothways whipsmart,
my buddies in high places,
my will of iron.

MESSENGER: AFTER THE FIFTH SPEECH OF THE MESSENGER, ACT 1, SCENE 3 OF HÖLDERLIN'S *SOPHOCLES' ANTIGONE*

You'd think this granite amalgamation
of hills would resist all earthworks,
but each and every day we hear the blades
hacking and lifting and cutting deep.
Where we thought a blank sheet
would be valley walls of Jam trees
and York gums and maybe the odd
grevillea, instead we got track marks.
Who's culpable in the internal combustion
addiction to add-on build out connect
rock-curve to flatworld skyline. Dogs
bark where roos have jumped, and if a stuck
record is the key to poetry burrowing in
then whose to put their hand up and take
responsibility for the flourishing
erosion, the silting of the engorged
brook after the grotesque downpour
getting too much of a good thing. This
braving of hot fences and spouts
of electric faith, a lone cow calling
low out of a Carlos Drummond de
Andrade poem no one here has read
at slanted noon. Heritage is hatched
with new generations of adaptations –
how might they accomplish realpolitik
in a backwater that's drying out
at any other time? Spouting
gerrymanders and ballot box
epiphanies, keelhauling this inland
valley towards contracts of silence

at what's witnessed. This calque
of a soul I ladle out on misbegottens.
Nonetheless, I want to tell my tale
however drab these Sunday soils.

AFTER HÖLDERLIN'S 'DER WINKEL VONT HAHRDT'
[THE DELL AT HAHRDT]

The bush is gone, but wheelbarrows
are arriving to staunch the wound – woodchips
of shattered trees, verdure's fragments
of ghost, market-failure's dissed commodity.
These causes that stem out of night,
canticles to dawns that are never
quite them same – but out of an enclave of hope,
where charismatic selves imagine a future of comforting
growth, belief is marked out, communicated.

FANTASIA ON HÖLDERLIN'S 'HÄLFTE DES LEBENS'
[HALF OF LIFE]

Lemon pears uplift to appear
Down on wild roses
While land enters the lake,
Swans love-struck
And hallucinating kisses
From stroking beaks
Under water, transcendent.

O, what reveals
Winter's grasp, the blossoms, and also
the sunbursts
and dirt shadows?
The wall's vertigo
crushing speech, implanting cold, while wind
smashes a weathervane.

FANTASIA (2) ON HÖLDERLIN'S 'HÄLFTE DES LEBENS'
[HALF OF LIFE]

Catchment overrun with sun-pears looming down
over dog-roses wrapping thorny arms around hell,
the dam mirror rippling with valley breeze
and black swans loving the chance
to dip deep into run-off, essence
of landscape stoned on forestry excess,
the foresters hallucinating trees no longer there.

And winter's replenishing hesitant
as *developments* narrow range down to a trickle –
flowers of sunshine low
on the horizon, ghosts of old tall-tree shade?
Concrete dam wall holding back
speech you can't drown out, can't flood
as the wind lifts and machinery gargles.

FANTASIA (3) ON HÖLDERLIN'S 'HÄLFTE DES LEBENS'
[HALF OF LIFE]

Low-hung pair of Apollonian fruits, luscious
To that wild rose season verging
As land into the lake,
Swans lusty with ecology,
High on fallout and toxic residues,
Dipping your heads, your necks,
Into the mixture with divine application.

I hesitate, as the new winter
Closes in on flowers, some sparking
In sudden warmth, sun resplendent
Through holes in someone else's ozone layer, burnt earth?
And so the mirrors rise-up
To throw back our speech, our denials, though silent
As the wind in phone towers, drones flying past fast.

LISTENING TO *NIRVANA* AND WORKING WITH ANDREE GERLAND'S 'LITERAL' VERSION OF HÖLDERLIN'S 'HÄLFTE DES LEBENS' [HALF OF LIFE]

With heavy, yellow pears
And replete with wild roses,
The land reaches into the lake,
You exquisite swans,
And drunk on your kisses
You dip your heads
Into sober, spiritual waters.

Pity me, for where can I collect
Flowers when winter closes in,
And where find sunshine
And earthshade?
The walls rise
cold and speechless; in the wind,
Weathervanes rasp.

AFTER HÖLDERLIN'S PINDAR EXTRAVAGANZA WHEN HE WAS SUPPOSEDLY PAST IT: 'DAS UNENDLICHE' ('THE INFINITE')

You see, I know, it's all about
walls towering and overpowering
and not just standing. They are never
still ± that's not equity, nor just
to be considered as such. The switch
across half-lives :: the uncertainty
of self comes to mind, laid out .

I am composed of ambiguities and I say so with precision.
Quoting the scales of justice, a humorist might ad-lib, 'The
contradiction is in the resolution.' For, you see, my grandfather
was a member of the Magic Circle, and beholden to its rules,
its secrecy. And that's where I come in, a third eye, an eternal
presence behind the scenes, marvelling at the slippages. Mine,
too. The case rests?

AFTER HÖLDERLIN'S PINDAR EXTRAVAGANZA WHEN HE WAS SUPPOSEDLY PAST IT: 'VOM DELPHIN'
[ON THE DOLPHIN]

And so, the river dolphins ingest the gifts of human toxins, small whitehorses nudging their baffled corpses.

When I hear a stranger – jogging along the path by the river – call out, 'See the dolphins!' and later, the sun askew through musty clouds, another ask, 'Have you seen the river-dolphins today?' I know the death of river-dolphins is immense to the humans who mark their lives by appearances and disappearances. Whether or not joggers connect their human actions to the sudden decline in river-dolphin numbers, I don't know. 'Nature' is a health-variable in riverside café discussions of river-health, and the very smell of water on a hot day is subject for debate.

Waves *do* occur in the river when storms clamp down on the coastal plain – dark-frothed white horses, the stained waters breeching the dolphins' trust.

AFTER HÖLDERLIN'S PINDAR EXTRAVAGANZA WHEN HE WAS SUPPOSEDLY PAST IT: 'DAS BELEBENDE'
[WHAT GIVES LIFE]

Tackle the ball not the man, counter
The Centaurs guileless and wanting
The violent cornucopia
Of booze advertising, tackling
Above the shoulder, around the neck,
The claret flowing, commentator, but celebrating
From the corporate cup, overflowing silver
Klaxons blowing, trooping the colour.

Centaur-identity so wrapped up around the Swan River with lip-service to Whadjuk country which is outside the corporate inner-circle, the sand of the plain transferring energy up through branches planted or self-seeded.

Wealth is the goal or points accumulating in Centaurville, the Perth Hills overlooking loss of territory, the bonanza of a premiership – tourism, the money flowing east to west, all angles covered that impossible kick from the back pocket.

Centaurs bodywork a sculptural science, a specificity of bodyform, and downfall through substances off script, left to run off the rails. Read about the fuck-ups as if, as if, all in the past. And then a career over, looking for that business leg-up, to make sense. Mates.

And down through the Scarp the river makes another river one and the same, renamed. From those towns, those colonial outposts through the Valley, players emerge to claim back but mostly to be claimed. Their fame outsources, though some manage to outflank. This story-telling from far away overlaying with Cyclops watching one-eyed over his sheep, the corporate raiders, the military advertising during peaktime TV, to protect the sanctity of the team of teams, the long-term recoveries, the permanently injured. And Centaurs wild at season's end, kicking up a storm, walking on 'red tides' choking the river, from stadium to ballroom.

And with beer in their bellies and approved supplements whirling through their bloodstreams, the Centaurs dance across the field, *AC/DC*'s 'High Voltage' smashing its way into the home crowd's identity banks, confirming this is one of ours, but then again, maybe it belongs to the Derby rivals, all that sandy coastline and fallout in the Sound, another club's claims to sponsorship? No, no, it's *Daddy Cool*'s 'Eagle Rock', and from the horn of plenty pours the history of a city, gatherings of the great inland catchment.

And so the colonisers burst out of the hollowed stomachs of the colonised. So Ossian is roped in, and Chiron who bestowed the secrets of the lyre on the warrior Achilles. And so for origins. And so for the drawcards. Sponsors lining up.

AFTER 'DER SOMMER' – 'WENN DANN VORBEI' DES FRÜHLINGS BLÜTHE SCHWINDET [THE SUMMER – WHEN THEN THE BLOSSOM OF SPRING VANISHES AWAY]

The vanishing of back-when's spring-flowers,
Summer's *now*, entwining the year.
And, as through the valley, Toodyay Brook –
The ranges at full-stretch to hold it back.
Paddocks are exhausted but glassy-bright
With day, arching towards twilight;
And so the year hangs 'round, a summer's
Day for 'men' as impressions might fade with nature.

May 24th
 1778.   Scardanelli

HYMN OF BEYOND HÖLDERLIN'S 'WIE MEERESKÜSTEN...'? [LIKE SEA COASTS...]

I am less associated with the sea than I'd like to be,
Says the sea god somewhat ironically, trailing off
Into the foam of immense breakers running
Out of steam, compelled by the revolutions
Of the planet, which, as you'd expect, drunkenly
Slops about its contents; but looking out
From the coast everywhere takes us short of a Grecian
Harbour, all those slaves rowing
Ships that could so easily break-up
On rocks, or sliding to a sandy anchorage,
Be leapt off – wading to shore, to hope.

WE, TOO – AFTER HÖLDERLIN'S 'WENN AUS DEM HIMMEL'
[WHEN FROM HEAVEN]

And thus from heaven downwards those bursts
   Of self-assurance we indulge as human,
      And thus we too take in all that's on view –
         Disturbance labelled 'sublime', an escape

From gorgeous immensity making songs of praise!
   And so we too truck with love as proof of top-dressing – lime
      From the pit spread as imagery compiles its inventory –
         And across the valley charred paddocks

Taunt emphysemic sheep nuzzling grubby soil
   While the burners dare fuck-faced drought to get a grip.
      And above us all, the wandoos lush with crown decline,
         The realms of husbandry OD'ing on vanity.

And thus the sheep are gathered, and thus the outcrops
   Bare their rough and unlipped teeth. And thus
      Laid bare the quail excite housecats stepping out
         Into the pastoral to confuse the card of instinct.

Which is not to say that the fencer working
   His Bobcat to make no man's land where Gender
      Has staked its claim and will go down swinging.
         Which is not to say the fencer doesn't pause

To admire the tree falling to his grunty little machine.
   And (or but?) there are cultivated trees glimmering – we
      Ourselves worshipping the lemon, the olive, the grape.
         But (or and?) manna wattles are raining yellow in dry weather.

And whose to say that Badiou's flurries of eventism –
His meditations on rivers and the Greek fantasia –
Aren't as *relevant* here as the *anachronistic* fence-
Post diggers whipped up by earlier 'landholders'?

DISTANCE IS HOW WE (DIS)ORIENTATE: AFTER 'WENN AUS DER FERNE...' [IF FROM THE DISTANCE]

Coordinates and proximities, distance
   Between two points, orienteering
      Out of our slumps, and through the haze –
         An inversion layer – the smiles via,

Then ID me and explain how such love comes to pass?
   Such glib revegetation of where great tuart trees
      Rose over landscaped futures, hanging gardens
         Consanguineous with river and flag raisings.

And so you were there, too, in a leap and a bound,
   A hop, skip and a jump away, your bloke
      All wrapped up in lightlessness, jammed
         Into stale shadows watching your warm

Gazes pass on through. But such moments
   Bestowed a weird calm on my flagrant soul,
      And I grasped measurement as epiphany?
         Yes! A declaration: unto you then always.

I swear it! And, as what was is reconstituted
   In our epistles of past joys and indiscretions,
      I am reformed in the stroke of a pen, the impact
         Of fingertips on *letters*, and I say it openly.

Was it spring? Was it summer? The crimson chat
   Comes in from the arid zone to fill our days, as those
      Introduced nightingales timidly sang in Melbourne
         A hundred and fifty years ago to change the tune

Of the antipodes – turn up the warmth – and perished.
    Botanical gardens unearth the local to make the world
        In our backyard, and we certainly walked under
            The canopies with bliss – *live and let live.*

Each morning across the gardens with the thinned river
    Flowing through, and back in the evenings to hear
        Darkness contracting the world's skin. And thus
            The enigma of our presence and intensity.

It's easy to let it flow into days of ensuring the farm
    Ran smoothly, the water flowing down from the dam
        As that young man found his feet among double-gees
            And barbed wire, leapt fences but only just

As his orbit decayed, and the few everlastings
    Growing on the edge of the woodlands crinkled
        With the sharp easterlies, those markers
            Vulnerable against their colonial naming,

The afternoon stuck at its centre, unable to dilate,
    Retract into the inland sea of desire. Accept, take
        Her happiness into your hours, drink in the sun
            And deny melanomas usurping its generosity,

Lifting truths out of us to grasp hands with grain
    In the silos, to promise season after season of growth,
        Only to be overcome by the fumes of pickling,
            The distance growing between us and the dirt.

And so my absence is an enunciation
    Of your isolation in the world! I love you,
        But you can't know all there is left,

BIOGRAPHICAL NOTE

JOHN KINSELLA's most recent volumes of poetry are *Drowning in Wheat: Selected Poems 1980-2015* (Picador, 2016) and *On the Outskirts* (University of Queensland Press, 2017). His most recent books with Arc Publications are *America (A Poem)* (2005) and *Comus: A Dialogic Mask* (2008). His volumes of stories include *In the Shade of the Shady Tree* (Ohio University Press, 2012), *Crow's Breath* (Transit Lounge, 2015) and *Old Growth* (Transit Lounge, 2017). His volumes of criticism include *Activist Poetics: Anarchy in the Avon Valley* (Liverpool University Press, 2010) and *Polysituatedness* (Manchester University Press, 2017).

He is a Fellow of Churchill College, Cambridge University, and Professor of Literature and Environment at Curtin University, but most relevantly he is an anarchist vegan pacifist of over thirty years. He believes poetry is one of the most effective activist modes of expression and resistance we have.

John Kinsella wishes always to acknowledge the traditional and custodial owners of the land he comes from – the Ballardong Noongar people, the Whadjuk Noongar people, and the Yamaji people.